IT'S TIME TO EAT TANGERINES

It's Time to Eat TANGERINES

Walter the Educator

Silent King Books
A WhichHead Entertainment Imprint

Copyright © 2025 by Walter the Educator

All rights reserved. No part of this book may be reproduced in any manner whatsoever without written per- mission except in the case of brief quotations embodied in critical articles and reviews.

First Printing, 2024

Disclaimer

This book is a literary work; the story is not about specific persons, locations, situations, and/or circumstances unless mentioned in a historical context. Any resemblance to real persons, locations, situations, and/or circumstances is coincidental. This book is for entertainment and informational purposes only. The author and publisher offer this information without warranties expressed or implied. No matter the grounds, neither the author nor the publisher will be accountable for any losses, injuries, or other damages caused by the reader's use of this book. The use of this book acknowledges an understanding and acceptance of this disclaimer.

It's Time to Eat TANGERINES is a collectible early learning book by Walter the Educator suitable for all ages belonging to Walter the Educator's Time to Eat Book Series. Collect more books at WaltertheEducator.com

USE THE EXTRA SPACE TO TAKE NOTES AND DOCUMENT YOUR MEMORIES

TANGERINES

It's tangerine time, hooray, hooray!

It's Time to Eat
Tangerines

A juicy treat to brighten our day.

Round and orange, so small and neat,

Tangerines are the perfect treat!

Peel the skin, it's easy to do,

The smell is fresh and zesty too!

Little slices, like tiny moons,

Sweet and tangy, they make us swoon.

Pop one in and take a bite,

The flavor bursts, oh, what delight!

So juicy, sweet, and oh so fun,

Tangerines are loved by everyone.

In the orchard, the trees do grow,

With tangerines that start to glow.

Farmers pick them carefully,

A yummy snack for you and me!

It's Time to Eat
Tangerines

Packed with goodness, healthy and bright,

Tangerines make us feel just right.

They give us energy to play and run,

A snack that's tasty for everyone!

Add them to your lunch or eat them plain,

Tangerines are sunshine after the rain.

In salads, drinks, or on their own,

Their cheerful flavor is well-known.

The bees and blossoms worked so hard,

To grow this fruit in the farmer's yard.

Now it's here for us to share,

A tangerine snack beyond compare!

So peel it slow, don't let it slip,

Catch every drop, don't waste a drip.

It's Time to Eat
Tangerines

It's sweet and tangy, the perfect pair,

A fruity snack beyond compare!

When winter comes, they're ripe and sweet,

The best surprise, a tasty treat!

Share them with friends, or eat them alone,

Tangerines feel just like home.

So let's give thanks for this juicy prize,

Bright and round, the perfect size.

Time to eat tangerines, what a delight,

It's Time to Eat
Tangerines

A little fruit that feels just right!

ABOUT THE CREATOR

Walter the Educator is one of the pseudonyms for Walter Anderson. Formally educated in Chemistry, Business, and Education, he is an educator, an author, a diverse entrepreneur, and he is the son of a disabled war veteran. "Walter the Educator" shares his time between educating and creating. He holds interests and owns several creative projects that entertain, enlighten, enhance, and educate, hoping to inspire and motivate you. Follow, find new works, and stay up to date with Walter the Educator™

at WaltertheEducator.com

www.ingramcontent.com/pod-product-compliance
Lightning Source LLC
LaVergne TN
LVHW052016060526
838201LV00059B/4047